PREFACE

With passion and drive, I was able to write something from my heart. My message to the world. I never considered myself to write or publish a book, yet here I am sharing my world with you.

These words felt a need to be heard, so I captured it all in this book, articulated to have each page speak for itself. If I had to describe this book in three words I'd use wisdom, freedom, and courage.

Embrace the journey, it's the most beautiful part of the experience.

INTRODUCTION

HAVE YOUR PRIORITIES STRAIGHT

Honestly what better way to start than with this? When your priorities are straight, it's literally like having a map for success. You know exactly where you're headed and what steps to take to get there.

With every day that passes, you keep yourself focused and disciplined. Don't be hard on yourself though.

The key here is to **want** to change. You can read all the books on the shelves, all the courses at your fingertips, and still not reach where you want to be. It starts with you. How much time and energy you pour into it.

You can lead a horse to water, yet you can't force them to drink it...

HOW BIG WOULD YOU DREAM IF YOU KNEW YOU COULDN'T FAIL?

If failure weren't even on the table, think about it ; it would be just the beginning.

And let's talk about the fear factor. Without that fear of failure lurking in the shadows, your creativity would skyrocket.

You'd dream up ideas so wild and innovative, they'd make the conventional seem downright boring. It's about unleashing your imagination in a way that's unbridled and unapologetic.

So, if failure were off the table, don't just think big, think game-changer. In this dream scenario, it's not about the 'what ifs', it's about 'why not.' Dream so big that failure isn't even on the radar.

Rewrite the script of what's possible and embrace the kind of dreams that leave a lasting impression on the world.

"Two roads diverged in a wood, and I—

I took the one less traveled by,

And that has made all the difference."

-   Robert Frost

PEOPLE WRITE BECAUSE NO ONE LISTENS

In the world of getting your point across, writing is like the secret weapon for those times when you're not sure if anyone's listening.

When you send a text, it's like you're giving them the chance to read, reread, and let your words sink in.

Talking, on the other hand, can be a hit or miss, sometimes it just goes right over someone's head.

So, writing becomes this intentional choice. You take your time crafting your thoughts, ensuring they land how it feels right. Writing gives your words a chance to linger, to be revisited until they resonate.

A form of expression making sure what you say sticks.

PER·SPI·CA·CIOUS

/ˌpərspəˈkāSHəs/

adjective

Having a ready insight into and understanding of things.

To a good friend, who has called me perspicacious once, and stuck with me. Navigate life with insight, make wise decisions, and adapt thoughtfully... Create a perspicacious mindset for personal growth and overcoming challenges.

Having this in your deck of cards makes you always ready to play.

PEOPLE AREN'T CREATIVE ANYMORE BECAUSE BOREDOM ISN'T A THING

In today's digital whirlwind, our constant connectivity has virtually erased boredom, the once fertile ground for creativity.

With endless distractions at our fingertips, we rarely experience the idle moments that used to spark innovative ideas. The instant gratification of a phone and constant stimuli might be stifling our natural creative flow.

In our quest for convenience, we risk forgetting that our most inventive moments often arise when we allow our minds to wander in the seemingly empty spaces between tasks..

YOUR MIND IS MONEY

The saying "your mind is money" comes down to the idea that what's going on in your head is like having a valuable stash of currency. Think of your creativity, smarts, and problem solving abilities as a kind of wealth.

In today's world, where ideas and innovation override, your ability to think critically and come up with unique solutions is like having a treasure chest of opportunities.

This is not always about academic knowledge, more how you use your brainpower in practical ways.

 Your mind is a tool for making things happen, whether that is in your career, personal life, or your overall growth. Just like you'd invest money to make more money, investing time and effort in developing your mind can pay off big time.

So, when someone says "your mind is money," they're telling you that your intellect and ability to learn and adapt are like a form of currency that can open doors, create opportunities, and pave the way for success in various areas of your life.

MISERY LOVES COMPANY

Sound familiar? "Misery loves company" speaks to the influence of those around you on your well-being. It means that the people you choose to be with can either uplift you or drag you down. If you surround yourself with negativity and discontent, it's likely to seep into your outlook.

On the flip side, choosing a positive and supportive company can have a beneficial impact, shaping your mindset and overall happiness.

A reminder to be mindful of the energy others bring into your life because, whether we like it or not, it tends to rub off on us.

PEOPLE CAN'T RUIN WHAT THEY DON'T KNOW

Keeping things under wraps until they're done is like guarding a <u>precious</u> secret. "People can't ruin what they don't know" captures the essence that sharing your goals or plans prematurely may expose them to skepticism or negative influence.

By staying quiet until completion, you safeguard your vision, shield it from external opinions, and ensure it blossoms on your terms.

It's not about being secretive... More about preserving your dreams until they're powerful enough to withstand outside pressures.

ONE MOUTH, TWO EARS

Ahhh yes. My favorite. The wisdom behind "One mouth, two ears" lies in the art of active listening. Our anatomy subtly guides us towards a profound truth: The power of listening outweighs that of speaking.

A reminder that conversations are not just about expressing what we know but also about absorbing the wealth of knowledge others bring.

When we engage with one mouth and two ears, we acknowledge that everyone has a unique perspective, story, or insights to share. Even if we possess knowledge on a subject we may already know, there's always room to learn more, to gain a deeper understanding.

Active listening fosters connections, opens doors to new ideas, and enriches our reservoir of knowledge.

This practice extends beyond words, viewed as an art about giving someone the space to be heard, understood, and valued. In a world that often emphasizes speaking, the power of attentive listening becomes a rare and impactful skill.

It's not just about "hearing", it's about comprehending, empathizing, and evolving through the collective wisdom that surrounds us.

"Most people do not listen with the intent to understand; they listen with the intent to reply."

- Stephen R. Covey

PERSPECTIVE IS EVERYTHING

Perspective serves as the lens through which we interpret the world. Comparable to viewing a piece of paper standing upright before us.

As we shift our standing point, the paper transforms revealing different angles, contours, and details.

Similarly, the way we perceive situations, people, or challenges is shaped by our unique perspectives.

In understanding that perspective is everything, we acknowledge the dynamic nature of <u>interpretation</u>. What may appear a certain way from one angle could be entirely different from another viewpoint. Our individual experiences, biases, and beliefs influence the way we see and comprehend the world.

Embracing the significance of perspective fosters empathy and a level of open-mindedness.

Let it encourage you to consider alternative viewpoints, realizing that a fuller understanding emerges when we appreciate diverse angles.

Much like turning that piece of paper to reveal its various faces, adjusting our perspectives allows for a richer, more comprehensive comprehension of the intricate narratives that surround us.

"Your perspective is always limited by how much you know. Expand your knowledge and you will transform your mind."

- Bruce H. Lipton

NOBODY IS COMING TO SAVE YOU

You were born alone, you'll leave this world alone.

Long story short: Nobody is swooping in to rescue you. Your journey, your dreams, your purpose, they're in your hands.

It's on you to shape the path you envision.

The world is yours to navigate, so take the wheel and make it happen.

THERE IS BEAUTY IN THE STRUGGLE

Life's beauty lies in its struggles. When things don't align as expected, there's a hidden purpose. It's a reminder that what you desire may not always unfold, and that's okay.

Embracing unexpected turns is where growth happens. The journey's imperfections, detours, and challenges add depth to your story.

Accept that the script might not match your expectations but trust that every twist has a reason, shaping you into who you're meant to become.

NO RISK, NO STORY

In life, it's simple: no risk, no story.

If you shy away from taking chances, you're left with a blank page, or two. The essence is in pushing boundaries, and trying even when failure lurks. Always.

The most remarkable tales are never born from playing it safe. They emerge from risking, stumbling, and rising again.

The beauty lies in the attempt, not the certainty of success.

So, embrace the risk, it's the ink that writes your story.

PRIVACY IS LUXURY

Privacy is a true luxury in a world where everything is often on display. The essence lies in not just understanding but embodying it.

Loving, being happy, making money, rebuilding, and even enduring losses in private is not secrecy, it is preserving the purity of these experiences. In a society wired for constant visibility, keeping certain aspects of your life private becomes a rare and precious commodity.

Safeguard the sacred moments, shielding them from external influences, and letting them unfold without the noise of judgment or expectation.

Few execute this because it demands a deliberate choice against the prevailing culture of oversharing.

It requires a conscious decision to savor the richness of life away from the public gaze, allowing personal growth and accomplishments to speak louder than words ever could.

Privacy, to a certain extent, is a deliberate step towards authenticity, where the truest versions of love, happiness, financial success, self renewal, and resilience can thrive.

Seek the understanding that some aspects of your journey are best experienced in the quiet corners of your existence, away from the constant buzz of external opinions.

THE JOURNEY MAY BE LONELY, BUT THE REWARD MAKES IT ALL THE WORTH

As you stay true to yourself, the road might seem a bit lonely, but there's magic to it.

Your authentic vibe attracts genuine souls, your people.

So, even when the journey feels like a solo ride, reaching your destination welcomes you to a community of like-minded individuals.

These are the people who see your true colors and make the whole journey way more rewarding than you ever thought. It's not about quantity; more about quality, finding your people and making the journey worthwhile.

DON'T LET THE MASK FOOL YOU

Don't be fooled by appearances; people are like icebergs, showing just a bit on the surface.

You only really get to know them when you've been through the ups and downs of money matters, travel, anger, or living together.

It's in those moments you see the real deal, beyond the masks we tend to wear and others hide behind.

A "RICH" LIFE DOESN'T ALWAYS HAVE TO DO WITH MONEY

Having a "rich" life is more than money, it's when you find joy in what you have, especially before success knocks.

If you're not content with the small victories, you'll miss the real richness of your journey when success comes knocking. Small wins are the stepping stones to the bigger picture.

True richness comes from <u>appreciating</u> the journey, savoring every moment, and realizing that happiness isn't a destination but a way of traveling through life.

FINANCIAL MISTAKES BY PERSONALITY

Great at Saving:

Excelling at saving is fantastic, but true financial wisdom involves investing to make your money work for you. Saving alone won't maximize your wealth; it needs to grow.

High Confidence:

Confidence is key, but it must align with your actual skills. Overconfidence without substance can lead to risky financial decisions. It's about marrying confidence with competence.

Cheap Spender:

While being mindful of spending is commendable, it's crucial not to confuse frugality with being overly cheap. Invest in quality when necessary and prioritize value over just cutting costs.

High Income:

Earning well is a blessing, but it becomes a curse if spending matches the high income. True financial success involves smart spending and strategic saving, regardless of your income level.

Highly Skilled:

Being highly skilled is an asset, but fear of judgment can hinder financial growth. Embrace your skills confidently, seek opportunities, and let your expertise contribute to your financial well-being.

Super Investor:

A knack for investing is impressive, but neglecting essentials like emergency funds can lead to vulnerability. Balance is key, being a super investor means considering all aspects of financial planning.

The essence lies in embracing a holistic approach to financial management. Each element complements the others, forging a path toward enduring financial success.

"Risk comes from not knowing what you're doing."
- Warren Buffett

KNOW YOURSELF INSIDE OUT

Knowing yourself inside and out is the core to personal mastery. To know yourself inside out is to navigate this terrain with authenticity and curiosity.

This depth of self-awareness empowers you to make choices aligned with your truest self, steering clear of paths that don't resonate with your essence.

In the pursuit of knowing yourself, you unearth the roots of your motivations, confront your fears, and embrace your aspirations.

"The best version of yourself"

Ultimately, knowing yourself inside out is a continual process, an ongoing dialogue with your own evolving identity. It's the key to living a life that feels purposeful, genuine, and uniquely yours, as you navigate the intricate tapestry of your existence.

"To know yourself as the Being underneath the thinker, the stillness underneath the mental noise, the love and joy underneath the pain, is freedom, salvation, enlightenment."

- Eckhart Tolle

HEALTH IS WEALTH

Health is indeed wealth, and it's not just about the physical aspect but the mental one too.

Nourishing your body with good food and self care reflects not just in your appearance but in how you feel.

Yet, it's a <u>50/50</u> deal, finding the sweet spot between going out and grinding.

It's the balance that's the secret sauce.

Your well being thrives when you've got both the physical and mental sides in harmony. It's not just a lifestyle, it's a genuine investment in your wealth, the kind that lasts a lifetime.

THE POWER OF NOW

The power of now is recognizing the strength you possess in this very moment. It's about not dwelling in the shadows of the past or getting lost in the uncertainties of the future.

Now is where your influence lies, where decisions shape your reality. A call to seize the present, channeling your energy into actions that mold the future you desire.

The magic isn't in reminiscing or worrying; it's in the immediate, in the choices you make and the moments you embrace right now.

So, don't just exist, live, act, and harness the power that resides in the present.

"The secret of health for both mind and body is not to mourn for the past, not to worry about the future, or not to anticipate troubles, but to live in the present moment wisely and earnestly."

\- Buddha

CHANGE IS GOOD

"Change is good" is a reminder that life's unexpected shifts, even when unplanned, often bring the most profound transformations.

It's acknowledging that to welcome new opportunities, you might need to close the door on the familiar. Think of change as the universe's way of <u>redirecting</u> you towards something better, even if it feels intimidating at first.

Closing a door isn't about shutting yourself off, sometimes you have to make room for the unforeseen possibilities waiting to unfold.

Every closed door signifies the potential for a new window to open, revealing a different view that might be more aligned with your growth and aspirations.

Change is the sculptor of personal evolution. It challenges, reshapes, and sometimes disrupts, but it's in those moments of uncertainty that resilience and adaptability shine.

"Change your thoughts and you change your world."
- Norman Vincent Peale

LOW EXPECTATIONS, LOW DISAPPOINTMENTS

Keeping expectations low is a shield against disappointment. It's not about settling for less, but about being realistic.

When you don't burden others or situations with lofty expectations, the chances of feeling let down are minimized.

By embracing this philosophy, every positive outcome becomes a pleasant surprise rather than an expected norm, making the journey more about appreciation than unmet expectations.

TALK IS CHEAP

"Talk is cheap" is a straightforward reminder that words alone hold little value without corresponding actions.

In the real world, actions speak louder than words. You can talk about a big game, but it's just noise unless you back it up with tangible efforts and results.

Words are empty air.

After all, in the arena of life, it's the doers, not just the talkers, who leave a lasting impact.

"Action speaks louder than words but not nearly as often."

- Mark Twain

LEARN FROM OTHERS MISTAKES

Learning from others' mistakes is like having a cheat code to life. You don't have to stumble on the same stones as someone else to understand the path.

Their wrong turns become your lessons, offering you a head start on the journey.

The art of wisdom is <u>recognizing</u> that growth doesn't always have to be born from personal missteps. By observing the experiences of others, you can navigate your course with a bit more insight, making the road a little smoother and the lessons a bit more profound.

After all, why wait to learn only from your errors when the world is a rich classroom, and every misstep around you is an opportunity for advancement?

BE A LEADER, NOT A BOSS

Being a leader, not a boss, embodies the essence of nurturing collaboration and growth within a team.

As an entrepreneur, the goal is not to dictate but to assemble a collective of individuals whose skills complement and surpass your own.

This approach isn't a sign of weakness; rather, a strategic move to surround yourself with diverse talents that can elevate the entire team. Working as a cohesive unit, where every member feels valued and empowered, leads to a shared sense of purpose and commitment.

A leader's role is to guide, inspire, and provide the tools for success, creating an environment where everyone contributes their best.

When team members are encouraged to share ideas and take ownership of their work, the potential for innovation and collective success becomes boundless.

The true strength of a leader lies in the ability to inspire and uplift others, creating a thriving ecosystem where everyone contributes their unique strengths toward a common vision.

WORK HARD, PLAY HARDER

Put in the <u>hustle</u>, reap the <u>fun</u>. When you've burned the midnight oil, and missed out on playtime, remember: that fun isn't going anywhere.

It's patiently waiting.

And when it's your time to play, you don't just play, you play hard. It's the sweet balance of grind and play that makes life worth it.

Work hard, play harder. Because that playtime is your reward for the dedication you poured in when the world was asleep.

Missing out on temporary fun over permanent stability is not missing out.

ALWAYS ACCEPT OPPORTUNITIES

Embracing opportunities means saying yes to the unknown, yet not allowing your comfort to be your downfall.

Opportunities, like rare gifts, often present themselves once. By saying yes, you open the door to growth, experience, and the <u>unexpected</u>.

Because the magic happens outside your comfort zone, where opportunities unfold and the extraordinary becomes possible.

"Opportunities don't happen. You create them."
- Chris Grosser

BRAIN VS HEART

The ongoing battle between the brain and the heart is a profound testament to the complexity of human decision making.

 Our brains, analytical and rational, often clash with the emotional whispers of the heart. It's a dance between logic and passion, a struggle to find an equal within the choices that shape our lives.

Alongside this internal conflict, there exists a divine intuition, an innate wisdom that transcends brain versus heart.

Like a silent compass that guides us towards what feels right, what aligns with our core values and aspirations. Trusting in this inner knowing is an acknowledgment that, deep down, we understand ourselves better than any external advice or societal expectation.

In the bigger picture, the key player is self-trust. It's the realization that, while the brain may offer logical analysis and the heart may express raw emotion, the ultimate source.

The decisions we make, rooted in this inner harmony, become a manifestation of our unique journey.

Trust yourself, for in the symphony of brain and heart, your intuition holds the melody of your truth.

"Trust yourself. Think for yourself. Act for yourself. Speak for yourself. Be yourself." - Marva Collins

FOR EVERYONE AROUND YOU TO BE HAPPY, YOU HAVE TO BE HAPPY

Ensuring your happiness is a vital step towards creating a positive ripple effect in the lives of those around you. Picture your happiness as the sun, radiating warmth and light. When you're content, that positivity extends to those in your orbit.

If you're carrying the weight of misery, it tends to cast a shadow on those nearby.

Misery does indeed love company, and the energy you exude becomes infectious.

Conversely, when you prioritize your happiness, it becomes a lighthouse, illuminating the path for others to find their joy.

Success in life isn't just about personal achievements; it's about having a collective sense of <u>well-being</u>.

So, don't see it as selfishness; view it as a responsibility to yourself and those you care about.

Your happiness isn't just yours alone; it has the power to uplift and inspire everyone around you.

CONFIDENCE AS THE KEY INGREDIENT

Confidence, when woven into our presentation, acts like a magnetic force. It's not a loud proclamation but a subtle assurance, a quiet belief in one's capabilities.

Others gravitate toward this self assured demeanor, interpreting it as a sign of <u>competence</u>.

The allure of confidence lies in its authenticity, attracting positive perceptions that go beyond the norm of surface impressions.

BE HUMBLE

Being humble is a powerful stance that speaks for itself.

It's about recognizing our strengths without <u>flaunting</u> them and understanding our worth without seeking constant validation.

In the realm of personal development, humility becomes a quiet force that opens doors and forges genuine connections.

"Humility is not a trait to be gained, but a posture to be maintained."

-John C. Maxwell

DON'T WORK FOR MONEY, HAVE MONEY WORK FOR YOU

The statement "Never work for money" reflects a profound perspective on the conventional notion of joining the rat race solely to pursue financial gain. Instead of working for money, the essence lies in making money work for you.

Simply working for a paycheck may create a perpetual cycle, where the pursuit of money becomes an endless endeavor.

True financial freedom comes from strategic investments, entrepreneurship, and building assets. Rather than being confined to the routine of trading time for money, one should consider how to leverage their resources. This involves investing in ventures, starting a business, and ultimately, creating a system where money becomes a tool that works on your behalf.

It's crucial to break away from the mindset that equates success solely with earning a paycheck.

The key is to transition from being a mere worker to becoming a creator and investor.

By understanding the value of putting money to work through various avenues, such as starting a company, hiring others, and acquiring assets, individuals can pave the way toward financial independence and long-term prosperity.

PURSUE YOUR PASSION

"Pursue your passion" speaks to the <u>transformative</u> power of embracing what truly inspires and fuels your inner fire. It's about recognizing that genuine success isn't a quick fix but a journey marked by experience and the courage to explore different paths.

Find your Ikigai.

By following your passion, you not only find fulfillment but also tap into your unique strengths and resilience.

When your calling calls, answer.

Discover what you love, and let your journey be guided by the authenticity of your passions...

"Success is not the key to happiness. Happiness is the key to success. If you love what you are doing, you will be successful."

- Albert Schweitzer

THERE IS NO SUCH THING AS "THE RIGHT TIME"

The <u>illusion</u> of 'the right time' is the enemy of progress. Riches aren't a result of fate; they're the product of decisive action. Waiting for the perfect moment is a seductive trap that hinders success.

The clock is always ticking, and the time is now. The difference between those who thrive and those who linger in the shadows lies in the audacity to act, to pursue dreams with unwavering determination.

In the grand scheme of life, the right time is the present, and success is the reward for those who make it happen.

"Do not wait for the right moment; make this moment right. Your destiny is determined by the choices you make, not the chances you take."

- Edmond Mbiaka

SILENCE IS THE BEST RESPONSE TO DISRESPECT

In the climb to the top, there's always someone trying to pull you down, often through disrespect.

It's a <u>test</u> – if you look down, you risk stumbling.

Here's the wisdom: silence speaks volumes. When faced with disrespect, responding with silence is a strategic move.

It keeps you focused on the climb, denying those attempts to derail you. Remember, sometimes the best response to disrespect is the sound of your continued success echoing through your achievements.

PROVE THEM WRONG

Proving them wrong is not just about defying skepticism; it's a declaration of self-belief and resilience.

When others cast doubts on your unconventional path or question your capabilities, it's an opportunity to rise above expectations. So, let them say it can't be done, and let your actions echo louder than their doubts.

The journey of proving them wrong is a testament to the extraordinary heights you can reach when you challenge the existing position.

"Prove them wrong silently, let success be your noise."

- Frank Ocean

THE ART OF NEGOTIATION

Negotiation in business thrives on finding a win-win balance. Clear communication, flexibility, and a focus on creating value ensure that both parties leave satisfied, having gained more than anticipated.

Successful negotiation is an art of collaboration, not contention.

Take it as a puzzle where both parties collaboratively craft a solution. Consider it fitting pieces together, creating value, and ensuring each side leaves with a complete picture of <u>satisfaction</u>.

ATTENTION IS THE NEW CURRENCY

In a world bombarded with information and endless streams of content, the saying "your attention is the new currency" captures the essence of how valuable your focus has become.

Think about it this way: when you mindlessly scroll through social media or get lost in a rabbit hole of online content, you're essentially spending your attention.

It's a currency that many businesses and platforms vie for. The more time you spend engaged, the more "currency" they gain.

This currency exchange isn't monetary, but rather, it involves your cognitive resources. Your attention is a finite resource, and every moment you spend on a particular app, website, or content piece is a transaction.

Companies and content creators strategically design their products and content to capture and hold your attention, often without you realizing it.

Moreover, the price you pay isn't just your time; it's the potential impact on your well-being. Constant exposure to attention-grabbing content can affect your focus, productivity, and even mental health.

Understanding that your attention is a valuable asset is the first step in reclaiming control over how you spend it. In this era, where attention is sought after like a precious currency, being mindful of where you invest it becomes a crucial aspect of navigating the digital landscape.

"The real problem of humanity is the following: We have Paleolithic emotions, medieval institutions, and godlike technology."

- Edward Wilson

THE FISHERMAN

There's a popular saying that goes like this:

"Give a man a fish, and he'll eat for a <u>day</u>.

Teach a man to fish, and he'll eat for a <u>lifetime</u>."

The message here is that many of us seek instant gratification, but what if I told you that you have the potential for both?

It's true, and it all comes down to your choice whether you want to depend on others for sustenance or empower yourself to be self-sufficient.

Ultimately, the decision is yours to make.

"If you want a thing done well, do it yourself."

-Napoleon Bonaparte

SHORT AND SWEET

In simplicity, there's a certain charm; keeping things short and sweet has a way of quietly captivating without you even realizing it.

With that being said...

IT'S ABOUT TIME

Now that you have accumulated the knowledge to have the "1%" mindset, it's up to you to apply it. As the remainder of the pages turn blank, it's up to you to pick up the pen and start writing.

Always remember this is your journey, your choices. The next pages turn blank and you are holding the pen.

ACKNOWLEDGMENTS

I am deeply grateful to all those who have believed in me, both now and throughout my journey. To those who <u>nurtured</u> the ground in which I've grown. I am beyond grateful. I trusted in the plan, and it has been blooming like a fresh flower in Spring.

Never doubt yourself. You fall down? Get up. Keep going and don't reflect too much on the past, it will never change. You allow things to define you as much as you sulk in it.

Every experience, whether positive or challenging, has contributed to shaping the person I am today. This is just the beginning, and I am thankful to every one of you who has played a part in it.

♥

THE "1″%" MINDSET

Notes:

Notes:

____

____

____

____

____

____

____

____

____

____

____

____

____

Notes:

____

____

____

____

____

____

____

____

____

____

____

____

____

Notes:

Notes:

Notes:

Notes:

Notes:

____

____

____

____

____

____

____

____

____

____

____

____

____

___

Notes:

____

____

____

____

____

____

____

____

____

____

____

____

____

____

___

Notes:

Good luck! ❖